PHONICS CONNECTIONS

Farming Then and Now

by Carol K. Lindeen

Table of Contents

capstone classroom

Farming Technology

How do farmers get milk from dairy cattle? How do farmers plant a whole field of corn? In the past farmers had to do these jobs with their hands. The work was hard and took a long time to finish. But today these jobs are a lot easier to do, thanks to technology.

Technology is the use of science to do something or to solve a problem. Over time technology has changed many things. Now one person can tackle a chore that used to keep a team of workers busy.

Imagine how hard it would be to plant a big field of corn by hand. Today special machines help farmers plant seeds faster than ever. How else has technology changed life on the farm?

Horse Power

Before farmers had the machines we have today, they planted and picked crops with their hands. Many of their tools were made of wood. Farmers used animals, such as horses and oxen, to pull plows and other heavy things. But even with animals' help, the work was hard.

A plow is a large tool that breaks up clumps of dirt. In the winter the ground settles and becomes hard. Farmers must loosen the soil in the spring before they can plant seeds. A plow cuts into the dirt and helps get the ground ready for planting.

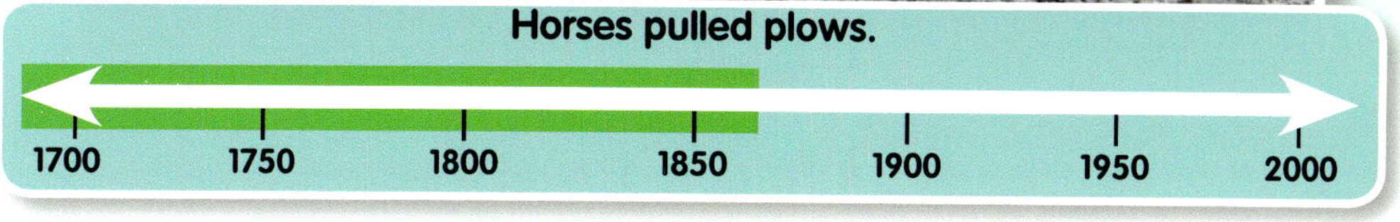

In the 1700s and most of the 1800s, a farmer would get horses from the stable and hook them to the front of a plow. The horses pulled the plow through the field while the farmer rode or walked behind.

The farmer held reins that were hooked to the horses' bridles. The farmer tugged on the reins to tell the horses to stop or turn. The horses did the heavy pulling, but the work was rough for the farmer also.

Sometimes dirt got stuck on the plow. Farmers would have to stop the horses to clean the plow. Sometimes the ground was so hard and dry, the horses were barely able to pull the plow through it.

Stronger and Faster

Walking or riding behind horses was tiring work. Plowing or planting a field was a slow job for many people. If only there were a machine that could help.

In the late 1800s, farmers tried the first tractors. These big, noisy machines ran on steam power. A boiler was used to heat water until the water was so hot that it turned into steam. The steam power made the tractor move.

Farmers started using tractors to pull heavy loads like plows. Tractors were stronger and could pull a plow faster than a team of horses.

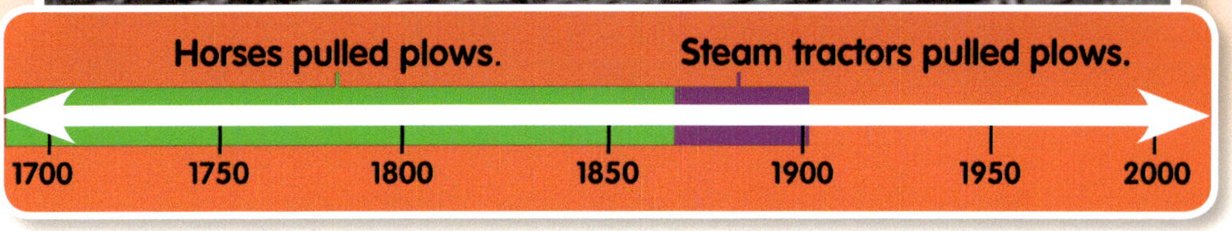

In many ways the tractor made farming easier. But the steam tractor was hard to handle. Also, heating the water in the boiler took time.

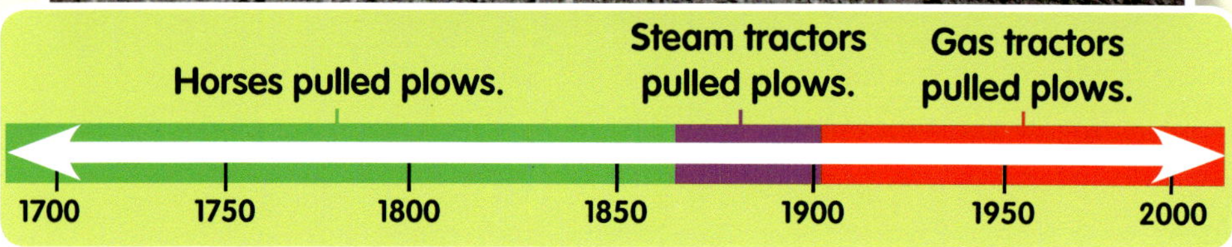

Around 1900 farmers started to use tractors that ran on gas. A farmer could start a gas tractor right away without heating a boiler. Gas tractors got stronger and easier to use as technology improved in the 1900s.

Today tractors have powerful lights so farmers can keep working after dark.

Horses can't walk very fast with a heavy plow dragging behind them. They also need to rest at night. But a tractor can keep moving as long as it has fuel. Today's tractors have more power than 100 horses.

Milking Cows

In the past dairy farmers milked their cows by hand twice a day. Farmers sat bent over on stools. They squirted milk from the cows' udders into a bucket. Milking cows by hand was a slow job. One farmer could only handle a small herd of cattle.

In the 1800s inventors looked for ways to make milking easier. An early system used tubes to drain the milk from inside the cows' udders.

Around 1900 an inventor made a milk pump that ran on steam. This led the way to newer, better technology.

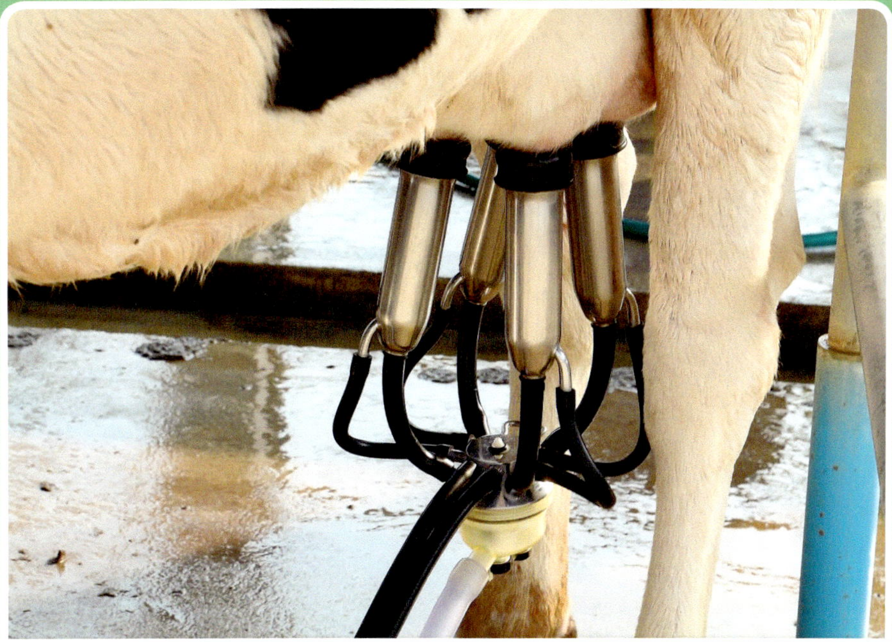

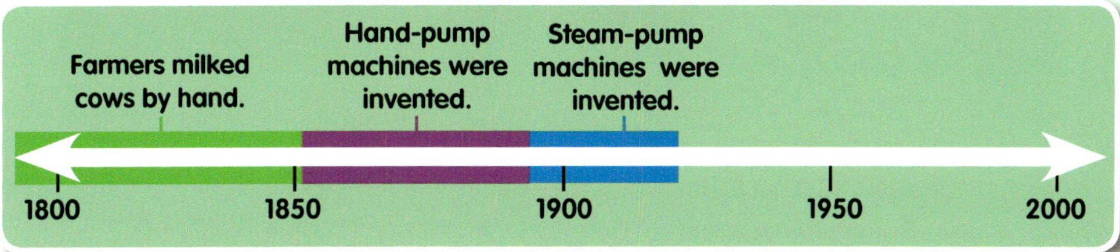

Today most dairy farmers use electric milking machines. A farmer puts suction cups on the cows' udders. The cups pull the milk out. The milk runs through pipes. A tank chills the milk until it goes to a factory.

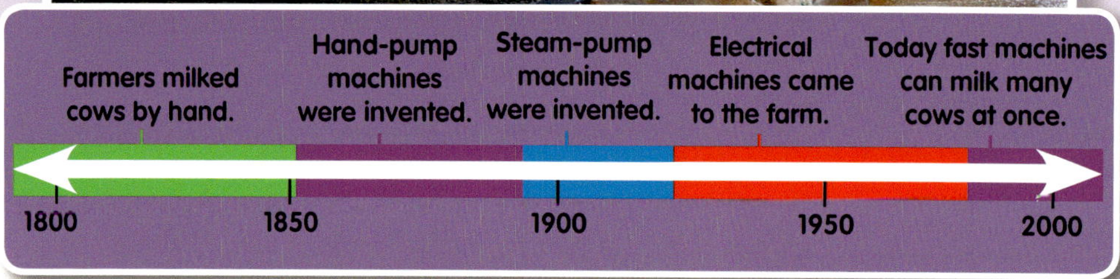

Modern milking machines clean the milk and keep it fresh. One worker can run as many as three machines. A single machine can milk 20 cows in 15 minutes.

Farmers today use technology in many ways to make their work faster and easier. Many farm machines even use computers and satellites. Just imagine what changes technology may bring to the farm in the future!

Index